*Children Demand a Verdict*

# Children Demand a
# VERDICT

## Josh McDowell
## Kevin Johnson

TYNDALE HOUSE PUBLISHERS, INC.
WHEATON, ILLINOIS

Visit Tyndale's exciting Web site at www.tyndale.com

Cover design by Chris Gilbert, UDG DesignWorks

Cover and interior illustrations by Eldon Doty

Edited by Betty Free Swanberg

Designed by Jenny Swanson

**Library of Congress Cataloging-in-Publication Data**

McDowell, Josh.

   Children demand a verdict / Josh McDowell and Kevin Johnson.
     p. cm.
Includes index.
   ISBN 0-8423-7971-1
   1. Apologetics.   2. Christianity—Miscellanea.   I. Johnson, Kevin (Kevin Walter)
   II. Title.
   BT1102 .M42 2003
   239—dc21                                 2003001147

Printed in the United States of America

07  06  05  04  03
6   5   4   3   2   1

# Table of Contents

**QUESTIONS ABOUT GOD**            Page
1. Why did God make people? . . . . . . . . . . . . . . . . . 2
2. How do we know what God is like when we can't see him?. . . . . . . . . . . . . . . . . . . . . . . . . . . . . . . . 5

**QUESTIONS ABOUT SIN**
3. Why do I feel bad when I do something wrong? . . . . 8
4. What if I don't feel bad when I do something wrong? . . . . . . . . . . . . . . . . . . . . . . . . . . . . . . . . . . . 11
5. Why does sin keep me from being friends with God? . . . . . . . . . . . . . . . . . . . . . . . . . . . . . . . . . . . . 12
6. Why does God say the punishment for sin is death? . . . . . . . . . . . . . . . . . . . . . . . . . . . . . . . . . . . 15
7. Why doesn't God just forget our sins? . . . . . . . . . . 16
8. Are "little" sins okay with God? . . . . . . . . . . . . . . 19
9. Why is sin sometimes fun?. . . . . . . . . . . . . . . . . . 20

**QUESTIONS ABOUT FORGIVENESS**
10. Why did Jesus die?. . . . . . . . . . . . . . . . . . . . . . . 24
11. Why did Jesus have to die for my sin when I haven't done anything really bad? . . . . . . . . . . . . . . . . . . 27
12. Will God forgive really bad people?. . . . . . . . . . . 28
13. Does God always forgive me? . . . . . . . . . . . . . . . 31

**QUESTIONS ABOUT GOD'S LOVE**
14. How do I know God wants to be my friend? . . . . . . 34
15. What kind of friend is God? . . . . . . . . . . . . . . . . 37
16. Does God love me more when I obey him? . . . . . . . 38
17. How can I be better friends with God? . . . . . . . . . 41
18. How much does God love me? . . . . . . . . . . . . . . . 42
19. How can God have time for me when there are so many other people in the world? . . . . . . . . . . . . . 45
20. Will God ever stop loving me? . . . . . . . . . . . . . . . 46
21. Does God like my sister more than me? . . . . . . . . 49

## QUESTIONS ABOUT PRAYER

22. Is God ever too busy to listen to my prayers?..... 52
23. Is God really interested in my problems?........ 55
24. Will God give me whatever I ask for when I pray? .. 56

## QUESTIONS ABOUT JESUS

25. Did Jesus ever do anything wrong?............ 60
26. Was Jesus ever tempted to sin?.............. 63
27. How can Jesus live inside me?............... 64
28. Was Jesus a wimp?........................ 67
29. Did Jesus know he was God? ................ 68
30. Did everyone in the Bible think Jesus was God? ... 71
31. Did Jesus actually die on the cross—or did he
    just faint?.............................. 72
32. Did Jesus really come back to life after he died
    on the cross?............................ 75
33. Could Jesus' disciples have made up the story
    about Jesus coming back to life? ............. 76
34. How did Jesus come back to life?............. 79
35. Is it okay to have Easter baskets and look for Easter
    eggs?.................................. 80

## QUESTIONS ABOUT THE HOLY SPIRIT

36. What's the Holy Spirit? Is he a ghost?.......... 84
37. How come I can't feel the Holy Spirit living in
    me? ................................... 87

## QUESTION ABOUT THE DEVIL

38. Is the devil real? ........................ 90

## QUESTIONS ABOUT THE BIBLE

39. How do some people know so much about God? ... 94
40. Why is the Bible so big? .................. 97
41. How is the Bible different from other books? ..... 98
42. Why did God put his words in a book?......... 101
43. How could God write a book?.............. 102
44. Who wrote down the words in the Bible? ....... 105
45. How do we know the Bible is from God?........ 106

46. The Bible is so old. How could it last so long? . . . 109
47. Are parts of the Bible make-believe, or is
    everything true? . . . . . . . . . . . . . . . . . . . . . . . 110
48. What will happen to people who don't obey the
    Bible? . . . . . . . . . . . . . . . . . . . . . . . . . . . . . . . 113
49. Why is the Bible so hard to understand? . . . . . . . 114
50. Why does the Bible have so many rules? . . . . . . . 117
51. Are the Bible's rules old-fashioned? . . . . . . . . . . 118
52. Is the Bible always right? . . . . . . . . . . . . . . . . . 121
53. Why are there so many different kinds of Bibles? . . 122

**QUESTIONS ABOUT DIFFERENT RELIGIONS**
54. Why do people from different religions sometimes
    fight? . . . . . . . . . . . . . . . . . . . . . . . . . . . . . . . 126
55. Does my Muslim friend pray to the same God I do? . . 129
56. Do I have to tell people about Jesus? . . . . . . . . . 130
57. Does it matter which God people believe in? . . . . 133

**QUESTIONS ABOUT RIGHT AND WRONG**
58. Can I decide for myself what's right and wrong? . . 136
59. Why do we need rules? . . . . . . . . . . . . . . . . . . . 139
60. Does God punish me when I do wrong? . . . . . . . . 140
61. Why is it sometimes easier to do things that are
    wrong than to do what's right? . . . . . . . . . . . . . . 143
62. How does God help me choose to do the right
    thing? . . . . . . . . . . . . . . . . . . . . . . . . . . . . . . . 144
63. Why do I sometimes get in trouble for doing the
    right thing? . . . . . . . . . . . . . . . . . . . . . . . . . . . . 147
64. Why do some Christians not act like Christians? . . 148

**QUESTIONS ABOUT THE FUTURE**
65. Does God know what my life will be like when I
    grow up? . . . . . . . . . . . . . . . . . . . . . . . . . . . . . 152
66. Does God care what job I have when I grow up? . . 155
67. Will God tell me what will happen in my future? . . 156
68. Why does God let bad things happen to me
    sometimes? . . . . . . . . . . . . . . . . . . . . . . . . . . . . 159
69. Can God make bad things turn out okay? . . . . . . . 160

## QUESTIONS ABOUT CHURCH

70. Why do we go to church?. . . . . . . . . . . . . . . . . 164
71. Why does church last so long? . . . . . . . . . . . . 167
72. My friend doesn't go to church. What should I do? . . 168

## QUESTIONS ABOUT DEATH AND HEAVEN

73. Why did my grandma die when the Bible says that Christians will live forever? . . . . . . . . . . . . . . . 172
74. What will I look like in heaven? . . . . . . . . . . . 175
75. Will everybody go to heaven?. . . . . . . . . . . . . 176
76. How long will we be in heaven? . . . . . . . . . . . 179
77. How do I know I'm going to heaven? . . . . . . . . 180

Index of Bible Verses . . . . . . . . . . . . . . . . . . . . . 183
Index of Topics by Question Number. . . . . . . . . . . . 187

# QUESTIONS
# ABOUT
# **GOD**

## Q: 1. Why did God make people?

A: God made us to be his friends. When God made the sun and the moon, the land and the sea, and the plants and animals that fill our world, he was pleased. But when he made people, he said that we were an extra-special creation. Why? Because he made us so that we're able to know him! We can talk to him and read about him. From the beginning of the Bible to the end, there's a clear message: God loves us, and he wants us to love him back. He wants us to trust him, enjoy him, and obey him. His plan is for us to live every minute as his friends. And someday he wants us to live with him in heaven forever!

**Learn It** Show your child the story of Adam and Eve at the very beginning of the Bible (Genesis 1:27-31). Point out ways we see that God was friends with Adam and Eve: God talked with them, provided food for them, and gave both of them someone they could enjoy being with—each other! Even more exciting is what the *end* of the Bible says about God's plan for us to be friends with him forever. You may want to read this special description of heaven with your child: "Look, the home of God is now among his people! He will live with them, and they will be his people. *God himself will be with them*" (Revelation 21:3; italics added).

*God looked over all he had made, and he saw that it was excellent in every way.* **Genesis 1:31**

*No one has ever seen God. But his only Son, who is himself God, is near to the Father's heart; he has told us about him.* **John 1:18**

## 2. How do we know what God is like when we can't see him?

A: We can't see God, because God is a spirit. He doesn't have a physical body like we do. God knew that it would be hard for us to understand exactly what he is like. So he came up with a wonderful way for us to know him. God, the Father, sent his Son, Jesus, to be born as a baby in Bethlehem. Jesus grew up and lived as a man—a very special, kind, perfect man. We can be sure that when we learn what Jesus is like, we will know what God is like. Jesus is just like God, his Father in heaven. In fact, Jesus *is* God! Jesus shows us exactly what God is like!

## Draw It

Read Luke 18:15-17 to your child. Provide clay or crayons and paper so your child can create a picture of that story. Talk about how kind Jesus was to the children. And name some things we discover about God by learning what Jesus was like.

# QUESTIONS
## ABOUT
# SIN

# 3. Why do I feel bad when I do something wrong?

A: You might *know* that you filled a bathtub with water that's too hot to climb in. But it's the way you *feel* that makes you jump out before you get burned any worse. In the same way, God planned for you to think about the way you *feel* when you have done something wrong. Doing wrong usually makes you feel far from God and from the people you hurt. Those sad feelings are a powerful message that you have done something that needs to be fixed. It's one way God helps you know you need to admit your sin to him—and do whatever you can to fix what you did wrong.

**Act It** Ask your child to playact this situation: "Pretend you did something wrong. Show what it looks like when you *don't* feel sorry." (Ideas: Make a face, stick out a tongue, and skip around as if everything is okay.) "Now show what being sorry looks like." (Ideas: Hang head down, look sad, and quiver lips.) Talk about this truth: "God doesn't want us just to *look* sorry when we do something wrong. He wants us to feel bad so that we'll admit our sin to him. Then he wants us to do whatever we can to fix what we did wrong, and we'll be happy again!"

*Yes, what joy for those whose record the Lord has cleared of sin, whose lives are lived in complete honesty! When I refused to confess my sin, I was weak and miserable, and I groaned all day long.* **Psalm 32:2-3**

*The law of the Lord is perfect, reviving the soul. The statutes of the Lord are trustworthy, making wise the simple. . . . By them is your servant warned; in keeping them there is great reward.* **Psalm 19:7, 11,** NIV

**Q:**

## 4. What if I don't feel bad when I do something wrong?

**A:** Some cars come with alarm systems. They are supposed to keep people from trying to steal the car or smash it up. But it's possible to unhook an alarm so it doesn't go off. That's what it's like if you pretend you don't feel bad when you've done something wrong. God created you to have an "alarm"—to feel bad for doing wrong. He did that to warn you away from sin. But sometimes you start to feel *good* when you do *bad*. You might punch your sister, for example, and smile about it. Or you might take a friend's cookie and feel good that you got it for free. Feelings should warn you away from sin, but feelings can also fool you. So God gave you his commands in the Bible. When you learn what the Bible says, you can always be sure about right and wrong.

## Share It

Share with your family how God's Word has helped you learn right from wrong. How has it been a better guide than your feelings have been?

# 5. Why does sin keep me from being friends with God?

A: God wants to be friends with each of us, but he is so special that he won't come near anything that's bad. So our sins make us God's enemy. The wrong things we do break God's laws, and they hurt the people God cares about. Since God only does what is right and loving and perfect, he can't be friends with people who don't want to be like him. And God, who does no wrong, can't allow sinful people to come near him. But God does want us to be friends with him. So he planned a way that he could fix the problem we have with sin. That's why he sent Jesus to Earth to die for our sins.

## Compare It

Say, "Imagine you were playing outside and your shoes were covered with mud. What might I say if you wanted to walk into the house wearing your muddy shoes?" Explain that you might say something like this: "I can't let you come into the house with dirty shoes. But I don't want you to have to stay outside forever. I want you in the house with me. So you have to take off those dirty shoes!" Point out that this is how it is with God. "Our sins keep us away from God, but he forgives us. That gets rid of our sins, just like taking off dirty shoes gets rid of the mud. When our sins are gone, we can be near God. We can talk to him whenever we want to because he is right with us."

*Your eyes are too pure to look on evil; you cannot tolerate wrong.* **Habakkuk 1:13,** NIV

When people sin, they earn what sin pays—death. But God gives us a free gift—life forever in Christ Jesus our Lord. **Romans 6:23,** NCV

## Q: 6. Why does God say the punishment for sin is death?

**A:** When our bodies quit working, we die. That's physical death. But there's another kind of death that is even worse. "Spiritual death" is when people are far from God forever and ever. It's the punishment people receive for their sins if they refuse to believe in Jesus. That sounds bad—and it is. When God says that sin leads to death, it shows us that sin is truly awful. It also shows us that God's free gift of forgiveness is truly awesome. Jesus died to take our punishment for sin. All we have to do is believe that Jesus is God's Son and that he died for our sins. Then, instead of spiritual death, we get God's forgiveness and eternal life with him!

## Compare It

As you walk through a mall or drive by a car dealership, point out some high-ticket items (a row of jumbo TVs, for example, or a car lot filled with new cars). Take the opportunity to say, "Those are really expensive items. They cost a huge amount of money. But Jesus paid an even bigger price to save us from being punished for our sin. He paid for our sin with his own life!"

# 7. Why doesn't God just forget our sins?

**A:** God would never lie. So he would never pretend that we're doing what's right when we're really doing something wrong. He wouldn't be unfair. So he wouldn't act as if our sins aren't a problem. He would never say, "Oh, that's okay. It doesn't really matter. Let's just forget it." Actually, there's something even better than God forgetting about our sins. It's God *forgiving* our sins! He wants to forgive us—to set us free from the punishment we deserve and to fix our broken friendship with him. The bad news is that God says there must be a huge payment for sin: death. The good news is that God sent his Son, Jesus, to pay for our sins. Jesus died for us and came back to life so that God could forgive us.

**Ask It** To help communicate our need for forgiveness, ask your child, "How would you feel if a classmate always pulled your hair and pushed you down but was never punished?" Then ask, "Do you think the wrong things that you do should be punished?" And finish with, "How does it make you feel that Jesus took the punishment for your sin so that you could be forgiven?" Talk about why forgiving is even better than forgetting. Discuss the fact that a forgiven sin is gone, not just forgotten.

*For God sent Jesus to take the punishment for our sins and to satisfy God's anger against us. We are made right with God when we believe that Jesus shed his blood, sacrificing his life for us.* **Romans 3:25**

*Now you are no longer a slave but God's own child.*
**Galatians 4:7**

# Q:

## 8. Are "little" sins okay with God?

**A:** Lots of people wonder if God gets angry at "little sins"—and we all have our ideas about which sins are little. We might think we can lie, gossip, or cheat without making God too mad. Wondering if we can be just a little bit bad, however, makes us miss the loving purpose behind God's rules. God hates all sin (Habakkuk 1:13), and that should be a big enough reason for us to stay away from sin of any kind. But there's another reason: God commands you to be good for *your* own good. Jesus died not only so your sins could be forgiven but to free you from habits that hurt you and others. Being bad—even a "little" bad—keeps you a slave to sin and makes you miss out on God's very best for you!

**Compare It** Use humor to point out the warped logic of this question by rewording it. Come up with comparisons like these: Is it okay to bang my right thumb with a hammer so long as I don't hit my left thumb? Is it okay to drink drain cleaner if I only drink half the bottle? Can I smoke if I only smoke a pack a day? Talk about how silly it is to ask if it's okay to do something just a little stupid. Point out that if something is bad, it's bad even if you don't do it too much. And if we really love God, we show it by not trying to get away with sins—even "little" ones.

# Q: 9. Why is sin sometimes fun?

A: Suppose you want a bicycle. One day you spot a hot new bike leaning up against a store window. It's unlocked, with no owner in sight. So you swipe it. You ride it home. You scream, "Wheeeee!" all the way. Well, getting a bike God's way—by saving your money—would have been slow, hard, and costly. Doing wrong just made it feel fast, easy, and free. Sounds fun! But sin doesn't stay fun forever, because people who disobey God won't escape punishment. God promises this: "Although the wicked flourish like weeds, and evildoers blossom with success, there is only eternal destruction ahead of them" (Psalm 92:7). Sin isn't as fast, easy, or free as it seems. It's not fun at all—in the long run!

Ask It Talk about these questions with your child: "When does sin feel 'fast, easy, and free'?" "What happens to sinful people in the long run?" Then talk about the opposite: "What good things happen when we choose to do the right thing—even if it's 'slow, hard, and costly'?"

*The way of the righteous is like the first gleam of dawn, which shines ever brighter until the full light of day. But the way of the wicked is like complete darkness. Those who follow it have no idea what they are stumbling over.*

**Proverbs 4:18-19**

# QUESTIONS
## ABOUT
# FORGIVENESS

# Q: 10. Why did Jesus die?

A: Who could take the punishment for your sins? A friend couldn't pay for your sins, because friends sin just like you do. A parent couldn't take your place, because even the best parents do wrong too. A pet couldn't die for you, because an animal could not take the blame for a human being's sin. Only Jesus could die in your place. He is the only person who ever lived who never sinned—not even once. There was no reason for him to die. Jesus is the Son of God, and he was punished for your sins—so you could be forgiven!

## Learn It

This is the most important part of the Good News. Jesus was our stand-in. He died in our place, taking the punishment we had coming. Here's another key verse to share with your child: "He was handed over to die because of our sins, and he was raised from the dead to make us right with God" (Romans 4:25).

*But he was wounded for the wrong we did; he was crushed for the evil we did. The punishment, which made us well, was given to him, and we are healed because of his wounds.* **Isaiah 53:5,** NCV

*If we say we have no sin, we are only fooling ourselves and refusing to accept the truth. But if we confess our sins to him, he is faithful and just to forgive us and to cleanse us from every wrong.* **1 John 1:8-9**

## Q: 11. Why did Jesus have to die for my sin when I haven't done anything really bad?

**A:** You might think of some sins as big and some as little. There's really no such thing. Some sins are easy to spot, like if you trip a friend. Some hurt people a lot, like if that friend falls down and chips a tooth. But all sins are wrong. God tells us that even every "little" sin is really bad. You also might think you don't sin very often, but we all do many wrong things. Here's what's important to remember: All sins are bad enough that Jesus had to die for them. All sins upset God, and even one sin hurts our friendship with him. Like James said, "The person who keeps all of the laws except one is as guilty as the person who has broken all of God's laws" (James 2:10). Being honest about your sins is the first step to understanding your need for God's forgiveness.

**Live It** When children think their sins are "no big deal," it often means they believe that the wrong things they do seem small compared to the terrible things others do. When your child does something wrong, help him or her pray a simple two-step prayer: (1) admitting sin to God, (2) thanking God for his forgiveness. Without owning up to sin, a child doesn't grapple with the wrong he has done. Without getting hold of God's forgiveness, he remains burdened by guilt. Your child can remember this two-step process by memorizing today's verse.

FORGIVENESS

27

# Q: 12. Will God forgive really bad people?

A: Jesus, God's Son, was known for hanging out with a tough crowd. He made friends with people who drank too much alcohol (Matthew 11:19). He talked with a woman that people didn't like because she had been married to many husbands (John 4:1-30). He spent time with a tax collector who had cheated a lot of people (Luke 19:1-10). So it's no surprise that God welcomes all people who admit their sin and accept his forgiveness, no matter what they have done. Jesus said that his goal is to save people who know they need his help (Mark 2:17). No matter who we are or what we have done, he wants us to remember one truth: All of us have messed up, so all of us need forgiveness.

## Act It

Whether we look "good" or "bad" to the people around us, all of our sins require the same solution. Ask your child, "If you were God, what would you say to us sinners?" Prompt your child to playact saying things they would say but God wouldn't, such as, "You're so terrible that I won't let you near me." "Your sins are too big to forgive." "Jesus didn't die for you." Then act out some simple scenes in which your child says some things God *would* say. For example: "I love you so much I planned a way for you to be near me." "My Son, Jesus, died for every one of your sins." "My love for you is bigger than anything bad you have done."

*We are made right in God's sight when we trust in Jesus Christ to take away our sins. And we all can be saved in this same way, no matter who we are or what we have done.* **Romans 3:22**

*He has taken our sins away from us as far as the east is from the west.* **Psalm 103:12,** NCV

# Q: 13. Does God always forgive me?

**A:** Maybe you stay mad for a long time when a friend does something to you that's unkind or hurtful. You don't want to be friends again until you make that person as upset as you are. So you treat your friend mean until he or she says, "I'm sorry" 1,000 times. The Bible has some great news: God isn't like that! When you trust in Jesus to take away your sins, right away he makes you friends with him again. And when you ask for forgiveness, he gives it! He forgives—the first time and every time after that—whenever you need him to (1 John 1:8-9). Not only that, but God *forgets* the wrong you do. It's as if he sends your sin off to the other end of the universe, never to be seen again!

## Compare It
Here is an analogy you can use to help your child better understand God's forgiveness: "Our friendship with God is like a beautiful vase. Sin is like knocking that vase to the ground—or throwing it at a wall. As humans, the best we can do is glue the vase back together and hope the cracks don't show. God does a far better thing. His forgiveness glues all the broken pieces of our friendship back together. We get a fresh start with him. A good-as-new friendship. It's as if we never sinned. All the cracks are gone!"

FORGIVENESS

# QUESTIONS
## ABOUT
# GOD'S LOVE

**Q: 14. How do I know God wants to be my friend?**

**A:** You can be sure that God is interested in being your friend because that's the whole reason why he made you. There are many places in the Bible where God calls you his sheep and tells you that you belong to him. Not only that, but God sent his Son, Jesus, to Earth because God wanted you to have a Shepherd to care for you. Jesus said, "I am the good shepherd; I know my sheep and my sheep know me—just as the Father knows me and I know the Father—and I lay down my life for the sheep" (John 10:14-15, NIV). God sent Jesus to give his life on the cross for you. God cares about you very much. In fact, he is your best Friend!

**Draw It** Have your child draw a flock of sheep and print the above Bible verse on the paper. Talk about ways a shepherd helps sheep and ways that Jesus, our Shepherd, helps us.

*Know that the Lord is God. It is he who made us, and we are his; we are his people, the sheep of his pasture.*

**Psalm 100:3,** NIV

*Lord, you are so good, so ready to forgive, so full of unfailing love for all who ask your aid. . . . For you are great and perform great miracles. You alone are God.*

**Psalm 86:5, 10**

# 15. What kind of friend is God?

God is a better friend than you can ever imagine. He isn't just kind—his name is *love* (1 John 4:7-8). He isn't just smart—he can count the hairs on your head (Matthew 10:30). He doesn't just own a big house—he rules the whole universe (Psalm 103:19). To help you understand how great a friend God is, think of all the people you trust most. Like your parents, who give you a home, food, clothes, and love. Or your friends, who make you laugh. Or the police, who protect you. Or your favorite aunt, who never forgets your birthday. God is like all those special people rolled into one, except he is far better. He is *perfect!* No one else is as loving, powerful, kind, and smart. He is God!

**Compare It** Have your child take a sheet of paper and write this verse at the top: "God is love" (1 John 4:8). List ways God shows his love to you. Then list people who remind you of God. Here are some examples: "God always loves me like Grandma"; "God gives food to me like Mom and Dad"; "God is always patient like my friend _____"; and so on. At the bottom of the paper, write these words: "God is the best friend of all!"

# Q: 16. Does God love me more when I obey him?

A: God wants you to obey him, so he is not pleased when you don't. But when you do wrong, God still loves you. In fact, he loves you just as much as if you had never sinned. God sent Jesus to die for you even before you told God you were sorry for your sin. Now, that doesn't mean God thinks sin is okay. God feels sad when you sin. He knows that sin hurts you and the people around you. God wants you to be safe and happy, and he knows that happens only when you obey his commands. So he will help you obey when you ask him. But he will never stop loving you no matter what you do.

## Ask It

The next time your child feels wronged by a friend or family member, talk about how sad and upset he or she feels. Ask, "How do you wish _____ had treated you? Why would that be better than how _____ did treat you?" Explain, "That's how God feels when we sin. He forgives us, but he still feels sad. He is upset when we hurt each other. He knows that obeying him is the best thing we can do."

*But God showed his great love for us by sending Christ to die for us while we were still sinners.* **Romans 5:8**

*The next morning Jesus awoke long before daybreak and went out alone into the wilderness to pray.* **Mark 1:35**

# Q: 17. How can I be better friends with God?

**A:** You can know *about* a famous person, but the only way you truly *know* that person is by spending time one-on-one with him or her. Your parents and pastor and Sunday school teacher can tell you all *about* God, yet what really makes you *know* him as a close friend is spending time with him for yourself. That's what Jesus did. He took time away from his followers to talk with his heavenly Father. He went to talk to God early in the morning (Mark 1:35). And he went often (Luke 5:16). When you spend time praying to God and reading his Word, the Bible, you feel close to him all day long.

## Live It

Is your child building a habit of spending time with God each day? If not, here's a simple way to get going: On small slips of paper write the references for Bible verses you want your child to learn—starting with short, one- or two-verse passages. Put these slips of paper in a cup, and draw a slip each day after dinner or before bedtime. Look up the verse, read it, and ask what that verse had to do with life that day. Ask about your child's "highs" and "lows" of the day, and pray about the things you discuss.

# Q: 18. How much does God love me?

**A:** Picture in your mind a sports fan who plunks down $1,000 for a sweaty jersey once worn by his favorite athlete. One day that shirt will fade and tear and be tossed in the trash. But the price that fan paid tells you he is nuts about his favorite player. Well, you have a fan who is even crazier about you. It's God! He paid a huge price to make it possible for you to become his child. He loves you so much that he sent his only Son, Jesus, from heaven to Earth. We celebrate Jesus' birth at Christmas. We thank him for dying on the cross for us on Good Friday. And we celebrate the Resurrection on Easter Sunday. Jesus' death on the cross is the price tag that tells you how much you are worth—a price so high it can't be counted. That's how much God treasures you!

## Compare It

Talk with your child about your family's most treasured possession—pictures, hobby equipment, your home, etc. Why does this thing mean so much to you? How would you feel if you lost it? Then explain, "We really value _____. But God's love for us is far more valuable. He loves us a zillion times more than we could ever love _____."

*You were bought, not with something that ruins like gold or silver, but with the precious blood of Christ, who was like a pure and perfect lamb.* **1 Peter 1:18-19,** NCV

*O Lord, you have examined my heart and know everything about me.* **Psalm 139:1**

## 19. How can God have time for me when there are so many other people in the world?

People can think hard about just one thing at a time. God isn't like that. He knows everything all at once! He has a perfect understanding of everything that's going on with you—and everyone else—all at the same time. Even though there are billions of people living on Earth right now, you are God's one-of-a-kind child. He saw you inside of your mom before you were born (Psalm 139:13-15). He knows your every thought (Psalm 139:2). He sees where you are every moment of every day (Psalm 139:3). He knows all about your future and has good plans for you (Psalm 139:16; also Jeremiah 29:11). Here's the best part: God not only *knows* about you—he *cares* about every detail of your life. Aren't you glad?

## Draw It

Read Psalm 139:1-18 together. As you read, make a list of everything God knows about you. Then encourage your child to draw pictures of some of the things you listed. This will be a great reminder of God's incredible care for each of us.

# Q: 20. Will God ever stop loading me?

**A:** Picture yourself enjoying a perfect day at the beach, running around in a special kind of sunshine that never bakes or burns you. Suddenly you get a nutty idea. You decide to run from that wonderful sun. You hurry inside, but you can't escape the sun's warmth. You lock yourself in a dark room, but light creeps in under the door. You discover that no matter where you go, the sunshine follows you. Well, you may or may not try to run from the sun on the beach. But God's love is something you *never* want to run away from. And you can't! God's love is like that special sunshine. It reaches everywhere. It never stops reaching out to you.

## Learn It

Read all of Romans 8:38-39—and make it your project to memorize this great passage as a family: "I am convinced that nothing can ever separate us from his love. Death can't, and life can't. The angels can't, and the demons can't. Our fears for today, our worries about tomorrow, and even the powers of hell can't keep God's love away. Whether we are high above the sky or in the deepest ocean, nothing in all creation will ever be able to separate us from the love of God that is revealed in Christ Jesus our Lord."

*I am convinced that nothing can ever separate us from his love.* **Romans 8:38**

*Remember that the heavenly Father to whom you pray has no favorites when he judges.* **1 Peter 1:17**

## 21. Does God like my sister more than me?

A: Think you know someone who's perfect? Here's a secret: He's not! You might think that God is more pleased with a sister or brother or best friend than he is with you. Perhaps that person always seems to do and say the right thing. But God doesn't have favorites. Here's why: Compared to each other, some of us might look better than others. But compared to God, no one looks good! Paul says that all of us have sinned and "fall short of God's glorious standard" (Romans 3:23). And Isaiah tells us that "all of us have strayed away like sheep" (Isaiah 53:6). We wander this way and that instead of following God and doing what he wants. The Lord knows that we all need his care and forgiveness, and none of us have it coming. The truth is, we all mess up—but God still loves us all just the same.

## Act It

Line up your family to compare who is tallest—and shortest. Point out that the differences in height seem like a big deal. Then ask, "What if we were standing next to a 100-story building? Would any of us look very big?" Explain that you would all realize you are very small and your differences are tiny. It's the same way with trying to see who pleases God the most. Next to him, none of us measures up, but he loves every one of us anyway!

# QUESTIONS ABOUT
# PRAYER

# 22. Is God ever too busy to listen to my prayers?

Sometimes the adults in your life are busy. You might hear a teacher or parent say, "Wait your turn." "Not now!" "After dinner." "Maybe this weekend." All of us know what it's like to have people tell us they are too busy to answer a question or to help us. Even grown-ups often hear from other grown-ups that they are too busy to talk or help. But that's not how it is with God. Just as there is no end to how much God knows, there is no end to how much he cares and wants to help you. God is with you all the time. He doesn't take naps or watch TV or surf the Internet. He never feels tired from running the universe. He is so tuned in to you that he knows your every thought before you think it. He's listening even before you speak. So go ahead and pray. Tell God whatever you'd like to say. Whenever you want to talk, he's ready.

Live It Make it a family practice to recognize that God is available to us 24/7. You can do this by practicing "popcorn prayers." As needs and concerns and points for praise arise, take time for brief prayers with your child. Explain, "You know, we don't have to wait until dinnertime (or family devotions or bedtime) to talk to God about that. Let's pray about it right now."

*Give all your worries and cares to God, for he cares about what happens to you.* **1 Peter 5:7**

*People, trust God all the time. Tell him all your problems, because God is our protection.* **Psalm 62:8,** NCV

## 23. Is God really interested in my problems?

**A:** Picture yourself as a first-grader sitting at the kitchen table working on a word list. The words aren't much harder than *ball* and *dog,* but you're having a hard time. Then your older sister comes over and says, "I can help you with that." Your sister is a big help because she had to do this when she was in first grade too. And she knows more than you know. God is like that, only better! Because God sent his Son, Jesus, to Earth to live as a human being, you can trust that he understands everything that bothers you. He wants to help you with your problems, and he has the power to do it!

**Live It** You can show each other God's always-available love by making a fresh effort to pay attention to each other's concerns. Here's one way to start: Talk about the fact that many of us do bad things to get attention when we feel others are not paying attention to us. Decide together on a positive phrase that family members can use when they need some help. When someone hears this phrase from a family member, the two of them should stop and talk to God together, asking him for wisdom on how to handle the problem. Try these: "I've got a 9-1-1 for God." Or just, "Can we talk to God about this?"

# Q: 24. Will God give me whatever I ask for when I pray?

A: Jesus said, "You can ask for anything in my name, and I will do it" (John 14:13). So Jesus did make an awesome promise to give us what we ask for. But that doesn't mean God is like a heavenly candy machine. You can't just put in a prayer, push the right button, and out pops your wish. When God hears our prayers, he always answers. But he knows what is best for us, so he doesn't always answer exactly as we expect. We need to remember that Jesus said to "ask in his name." To ask in the name of Jesus means to tell God you want things that will bring him glory. What does that mean? It means that God will get the credit as we praise him for answering our prayers. So he answers in a way that shows how great he is. He answers by doing things that are good for us and all the other people in the world.

## Ask It

Your child needs to know that God is eager to hear about our hurts, needs, and desires. But talk with your child about this question: "How can we pray so we aren't treating God like a candy machine? What can we ask for that would be good for us and all the other people in our lives—and bring God glory?"

*You can ask for anything in my name, and I will do it,*
*because the work of the Son brings glory to the Father.*
*Yes, ask anything in my name, and I will do it!*

**John 14:13-14**

# QUESTIONS
# ABOUT
# JESUS

# Q: 25. Did Jesus ever do anything wrong?

A: We must never picture Jesus as just another super-nice person, like a girl or boy at school who never talks out of turn or cuts into line. Jesus isn't just pretty good. He's the Son of God, and he's perfect! When the enemies of Jesus wanted a reason to put him on the cross to die, they tried hard to find bad things he had done. They couldn't find any! So they asked people to lie and say bad things about Jesus (Matthew 26:59). But Peter said, "He never sinned" (1 Peter 2:22) and he is "the sinless, spotless Lamb of God" (1 Peter 1:19). Hebrews adds that he "did not sin" (4:15). Jesus always did what was right. He obeyed his Father perfectly, so he is a perfect example for us.

## Ask It

Ask your child, "How does it make you feel knowing that Jesus never did anything wrong? How does it help you to know that Jesus was perfect?" Talk about the fact that Jesus became our Savior when he died on the cross. But during the time when he was alive on Earth, he also was a wonderful example for us. The Bible tells us to "fix our eyes on Jesus" (Hebrews 12:2, NIV). That means we should look at what Jesus did and learn to be like him.

*The chief priests and the whole Sanhedrin were looking for false evidence against Jesus so that they could put him to death. But they did not find any.* **Matthew 26:59-60,** NIV

[Jesus] understands our weaknesses, for he faced all of
the same temptations we do, yet he did not sin. So let us
come boldly to the throne of our gracious God. There we
will receive his mercy, and we will find grace to help us
when we need it. **Hebrews 4:15-16**

# Q: 26. Was Jesus ever tempted to sin?

**A:** Yep! The devil himself once tempted Jesus to show off his powers (Matthew 4:1-11). The Bible also says that Jesus "faced all of the same temptations we do" (Hebrews 4:15). Temptation is a powerful pull to do something wrong. It's such a pesky part of everyday life that Jesus would not have been human if he had never felt tempted. Jesus was God, but he was also human like you and me. He faced the same strong tugs to do wrong that we do, but here's the difference: When you and I are tempted, we often give in. Jesus never did. That's great news. You can be sure Jesus understands what a struggle it is to keep from doing wrong. But you can also be sure he will help you keep from giving in to temptation!

## Act It

Ask your child if she can name some temptations she faces in everyday life. Then read 1 Corinthians 10:13, which promises that in the midst of a temptation God always provides a way out. Role-play some temptations your child faces, pointing out how she can always ask Jesus for help by praying anywhere at any time. Name some ways Jesus might help your child escape powerful pulls to do wrong, such as providing a friend who also doesn't want to give in to temptation.

# Q: 27. How can Jesus live inside me?

A: When you hear people say that Jesus "lives in your heart" it doesn't mean you have an itsy-bitsy man camping inside you. It means that when you trust in Jesus, he is present in your life. But he isn't just with you. He is so close that he is inside you. Now, it's a mystery exactly how Jesus can live inside each Christian, but we do know that he made this promise to his followers before he returned to heaven: "I am with you always" (Matthew 28:20). Each time you let Jesus help you obey God, you make him more and more welcome in your life. It's important to obey him when he helps you know in your heart what's the right thing to do. Jesus Christ living in you makes you a strong Christian!

## Share It
Talk with your child about how you have sensed Jesus living in you, helping you understand and obey God. Perhaps you want to tell how he helped you make the right decision about what to study, what job to take, who to marry, where to live, where to go to church, how to be obedient to God in a difficult situation, and so on.

*And I pray that Christ will be more and more at home in your hearts as you trust in him.* **Ephesians 3:17**

*Jesus grew both in height and in wisdom, and he was loved by God and by all who knew him.* **Luke 2:52**

# Q: 28. Was Jesus a wimp?

A: Some pictures of Jesus make him look pale and weak—like someone who maybe got beat up a lot growing up in his hometown of Nazareth. We don't know what Jesus looked like. It's true that he was a gentle poet and storyteller who bounced children on his knee. He helped sick people and those who were hungry and thirsty. But he also had the rough hands of a carpenter. He was able to live alone for a long time in the wilderness. He knocked over the tables of cheating businessmen. Then he was willing to go through a difficult death on the cross, but he also had the power to come back to life. Can you picture him? Jesus is tender enough to care for your every need. But he is tough enough to be your all-powerful Savior.

## Ask It

Read the passage above to your child, then ask, "What do you think it was like to grow up around Jesus?" Follow up with this: "What qualities do you think made Jesus lovable to both God and people? What does the Bible tell us about the kind of person Jesus was?"

## 29. Did Jesus know he was God?

**A:** Many non-Christians agree that Jesus was one of the most important leaders who ever walked the Earth. They admit he was an excellent teacher of right and wrong—and an especially good person. Jesus, however, claimed to be much more. He said he was God! Listen to this example, just one of many in the New Testament. Jesus said, "The Father and I are one" (John 10:30). The religious leaders understood exactly what he meant. They shouted, "You, a mere man, have made yourself God" (John 10:33). They picked up rocks to throw at him, trying to kill him. To everyone around Jesus, his claim to be God was shocking—shockingly clear!

**Learn It** Explain that in this instance *blasphemy* means claiming to be God when you're just a human person. But Jesus *is* God, and he knew it. Read Philippians 2:6-11, where we hear the promise that one day we will all bow to Jesus. Talk about what a sad day that will be for those who never believed that Jesus is who he said he is. They will bow down to Jesus, not because they love him, but because they have to finally admit he is God. What a great day, though, for all of us who do believe that Jesus is God's Son! We'll be able to love and worship him forever.

Jesus said, "At my Father's direction I have done many things to help the people. For which one of these good deeds are you killing me?" They replied, "Not for any good work, but for blasphemy, because you, a mere man, have made yourself God." **John 10:32-33**

*Even in his own land and among his own people, he was not accepted. But to all who believed him and accepted him, he gave the right to become children of God.*

**John 1:11-12**

# Q: 30. Did everyone in the Bible think Jesus was God?

A: It's sad, but not everyone who met Jesus recognized him as God's Son, who came to be the Savior of the world. They should have! After all, God had said for hundreds of years that he would send a Savior to free his people from sin. The Old Testament has many special promises called prophecies. Long before Jesus was born, these prophecies described what the Savior would be like. He would be born in Bethlehem (Micah 5:2), do miracles (Isaiah 35:5-6), be betrayed by a friend (Psalm 41:9), have his hands and feet pierced (Psalm 22:16), suffer and die for our sins (Isaiah 53:5), and rise from the dead (Psalm 16:10). Jesus perfectly fit not just a few, but hundreds of prophecies spoken hundreds of years before his birth. To anybody willing to see, this was powerful proof that Jesus was who he claimed to be!

## Compare It
The probability of one person fulfilling even 48 major prophecies, according to Peter Stoner in *Science Speaks,* is 1 in 10 to the 157th power. That's the number 10 followed by 157 zeroes. The chance of someone fulfilling just eight prophecies is 1 in 10 to the 17th power. Share this picture with your child: "The chance that Jesus would fulfill just eight out of hundreds of prophecies is the same as the chance that you could find one marked silver dollar out of a pile of silver dollars in a pile two feet deep covering the whole state of Texas!"

## Q: 31. Did Jesus actually die on the cross—or did he just faint?

A: When Jesus rose from the dead, it was a one-of-a-kind event. It was so out of the ordinary that many people have said it couldn't possibly have happened. In fact, some say Jesus never even died on the cross. He just fainted, and in the cool air of the tomb he woke up and walked out. But that's impossible to believe when you understand what Jesus went through the day he died. First the soldiers beat him. Then they nailed him to a cross. He hung there for six hours before he died. He was taken down from the cross only after a Roman soldier promised the Roman governor that he was dead. We can be sure that Jesus died. And we can be certain he came back to life.

## Learn It

Talk with your family about the fact that if we get rid of the Resurrection, we get rid of Christianity. That's why so many non-Christians have tried to prove that Jesus never rose. No wonder Paul said we would be "the most miserable people in the world" if Christ were not alive (1 Corinthians 15:19). We would face all the trials, struggles, and problems of the Christian life—and then die with no hope of heaven. Thank God that he had a better plan!

*God raised Jesus from the dead, and if God's Spirit is living in you, he will also give life to your bodies that die. God is the One who raised Christ from the dead, and he will give life through his Spirit that lives in you.* **Romans 8:11,** NCV

*I passed on to you what was most important and what had also been passed on to me—that Christ died for our sins, just as the Scriptures said. He was buried, and he was raised from the dead on the third day, as the Scriptures said.* **1 Corinthians 15:3-4**

# Q: 32. Did Jesus really come back to life after he died on the cross?

A: Can you imagine a more astonishing miracle than a dead man coming back to life? The Bible tells us several big facts about the totally real rising again, or "resurrection," of Jesus. First, Jesus died (John 19:28-37). Second, Jesus was buried (Luke 23:53). Third, Jesus really rose from the dead! You probably know that Jesus' closest friends found his empty tomb (Luke 24:1-7). Later his closest friends saw him alive (Luke 24:35-49). But did you know that Jesus also appeared to hundreds of people in his fully alive body (1 Corinthians 15:6)? Jesus wanted people to know his resurrection wasn't a crazy, made-up story. He wanted to make it easy, even for us today, to believe that he is alive.

## Learn It
Help your child summarize the events of Holy Week as described in the Gospels. Most children easily accept the Resurrection as a fact. But if your child raises questions you can't answer, look for more in-depth answers in *More than a Carpenter* (Tyndale House Publishers, 1987) and *The New Evidence That Demands a Verdict* (Thomas Nelson, 1999).

# Q:

## 33. Could Jesus' disciples have made up the story about Jesus coming back to life?

# A:

If you wanted to know whether or not the moon is made of cheese, you would try to get information from people you could trust. You would need to hear the same facts from loads of people who had actually had a picnic on the moon, right? But what would make you really believe the truth would be finding people willing to die for their story—because people aren't willing to die for a lie. That's the kind of wonderful proof we have that Jesus rose from the dead. Many people saw Jesus alive. They all reported the same facts. And each of them faced the danger of death for spreading the Good News about Jesus. The disciples didn't make up their story. They were star witnesses to the truth!

## Learn It

Read in Matthew 28:11-15 about the efforts people made right from the start to disprove the Resurrection. Talk with your child about why the leaders in the passage didn't want to believe that Jesus was alive. Explain that these leaders wanted people to follow them instead of Jesus.

*This is that disciple who saw these events and recorded them here. And we all know that his account of these things is accurate.* **John 21:24**

*Jesus Christ our Lord was shown to be the Son of God when God powerfully raised him from the dead by means of the Holy Spirit.* **Romans 1:4**

# Q: 34. How did Jesus come back to life?

A: When Jesus came back to life, it was an event that was completely different from anything that had ever happened. A dead person had never before had the power to come to life and leave his grave. Lazarus had come out of his grave (John 11:38-44). But he hadn't done it alone—it was through Jesus' power. After Jesus' body was placed in a tomb, we can be sure *what* happened—Jesus left the tomb, so it was empty. We know all about *who* did it—our Savior, Jesus. The Bible clearly explains *why* Jesus came back to life—this event provides proof of who he is. But *how* did Jesus do it? That's a mystery. In fact, it's a miracle! The Bible does say that God the Father raised up Jesus through the power of the Holy Spirit. The Spirit of God is the only power in the world big enough to win the battle over death.

## Compare It
We don't have to understand exactly how God raised his Son, Jesus, from the dead to know that Jesus is truly alive. Most of us don't really know how cars work, yet we ride in them. Most of us don't have a clue how computers work, yet we use them and sometimes crash them! Even if we don't always understand the working of the Spirit, the amazing news is that the same power that raised Jesus from the dead will raise us to life in heaven (Romans 8:11)!

# Q: 35. Is it okay to have Easter baskets and look for Easter eggs?

A: You dart behind a tree, pull apart the grass, and pop open a plastic egg. Out falls a bunch of jelly beans. Sounds fun! But people sometimes wonder if it's an okay thing to do on Easter. Any other day of the year it would be tough to knock a visit from a bunny that brings candy. Yet here's the problem: Sometimes the Easter Bunny turns into a bigger deal than Jesus—just like Santa Claus can crowd out the true message of Christmas. In whatever way your family celebrates Easter, your big job is to make Jesus the big deal. Easter is your special day to remember that Jesus rose from the dead. And that's even better than a basketful of jumbo-size chocolate bunnies!

## Ask It

Each family needs to make up its own mind about how to keep Christ at the center of the holidays. Ask your child, "How well do we do in remembering that Easter is about Jesus? Is there anything we want to do differently?" Read the verses from Matthew 28 again and talk about what a joyful message the angel had for the women. No matter how your family celebrates, it's important to be joyful over the Good News of the Resurrection.

Then the angel spoke to the women. "Don't be afraid!" he said. "I know you are looking for Jesus, who was crucified. He isn't here! He has been raised from the dead, just as he said would happen." **Matthew 28:5-6**

# QUESTIONS
# ABOUT
# THE HOLY SPIRIT

# Q: 36. What's the Holy Spirit? Is he a ghost?

A: It might seem hard to understand what the Holy Spirit is like, but here's the big fact to remember: The Holy Spirit is God—along with God the Father and God the Son. Even though some Bibles call the Holy Spirit the "Holy Ghost," he isn't a ghost like you see in a cartoon or spooky movie. He's real and he's alive. He just doesn't have a body, so we can't see him. We say the Spirit of God is holy because he is perfect and pure, just like the Father and the Son.

## Learn It

Help your child understand that God as Father, Son, and Holy Spirit has always been around. Even at Creation, "the Spirit of God was hovering over" the formless Earth (Genesis 1:2). The Holy Spirit is present throughout the Old Testament (see, for example, Judges 3:10 and Micah 3:8). He is at the baptism of Jesus (Luke 3:22). Jesus said the Spirit would come to be with his disciples after he returned to the Father (John 14:15-17), a promise that was fulfilled at Pentecost (Acts 2:1-4).

*I will ask the Father, and he will give you another Helper to be with you forever—the Spirit of truth.*

**John 14:16-17,** NCV

*When the Holy Spirit controls our lives, he will produce this kind of fruit in us: love, joy, peace, patience, kindness, goodness, faithfulness, gentleness, and self-control.*

**Galatians 5:22-23**

# Q: 37. How come I can't feel the Holy Spirit living in me?

A: You can't see the wind, but you can see it sway the trees. You can't see the Holy Spirit, but you can tell that he is at work inside you. His presence in everyone who believes in Jesus is a fact (Ephesians 1:13). And look at some of the great ways you can watch him help you grow: He makes you sure that God loves you (Romans 5:5). He helps you know Jesus better (Ephesians 3:19). He sets you free from sin (Romans 8:2). He teaches you right from wrong (John 16:8) and builds character in you (Galatians 5:22-23). He equips you with talents, abilities, and spiritual gifts so you can serve God (1 Corinthians 12:4, 11). When you see those things beginning to happen in you, that's proof that the Holy Spirit is present in your life.

## Live It

Do you want to see more of the Holy Spirit's work in your family? Pray the following prayer from Ephesians 3:16-19. You may want to pray it aloud for your family members at least once a week. "I pray that from his glorious, unlimited resources [God] will give you mighty inner strength through his Holy Spirit. And I pray that Christ will be more and more at home in your hearts as you trust in him. May your roots go down deep into the soil of God's marvelous love. And may you have the power to understand, as all God's people should, how wide, how long, how high, and how deep his love really is. . . . Then you will be filled with the fullness of life and power that comes from God."

# QUESTION
## ABOUT
# THE DEVIL

# Q: 38. Is the devil real?

A: The devil (also called "Satan") is one of the first characters we meet in the Bible. He shows up as a serpent in the Garden of Eden to tempt Adam and Eve. He tells them it's okay to disobey God (Genesis 3:1-15). Some people picture the devil as nothing more than a fun-loving cartoon character with horns and long, red underwear, but he is very real. He wants to be powerful like God, and he wants us to join his fight against God. One of his big goals is to get people to sin. He tries to make *good* look bad and *bad* look good. But the Bible has great news: "God's Spirit, who is in you, is greater than the devil, who is in the world" (1 John 4:4, NCV). That means the Holy Spirit can stop you from giving in to the devil's temptations. When you pray, the devil runs away!

## Learn It

The devil is real, but he shouldn't be a fearful focus for your child. God's love and power are far better realities to fill your child's mind. If your child worries about the devil you can say, "Yes, the devil is real, and he is scary. But when we became Christians, we chased him out of our lives. He's not anywhere near as strong as God, so we can trust God to protect us."

*Resist the Devil, and he will flee from you. Draw close to God, and God will draw close to you.* **James 4:7-8**

# QUESTIONS
## ABOUT
# THE BIBLE

# Q: 39. How do some people know so much about God?

**A:** Suppose you want to know all there is to know about the goliath bird-eating spider *(Theraphosa blondi),* the world's largest spider. You would fly to the jungles of South America for a firsthand look at these hairy 11- to 12-inch monsters. You would study how they eat—and how they swallow. You might bring a baby spider home to your lab. Well, if you want to know all about God, you need to try just as hard to see what you can learn. You read the Bible. You talk to God day by day about your struggles. You say thanks for God's gifts, obey him even when it's hard, and trust him to care for you always. You learn everything you can about God's Son, because he is just like his Father in heaven. There's no doubt about it: Soon you will know God very well. And his Son, Jesus, will not only be your Savior and your Master but your best Friend.

**Live It** Talk about what you are doing each day to learn more about God. (Reading this book counts!) Pull out your family calendar: What might get in your way so you don't have time to learn to know God better? Choose one or two things each family member can do to learn more about God.

*I no longer call you servants, because a master doesn't confide in his servants. Now you are my friends.*

**John 15:15**

*Jesus' disciples saw him do many other miraculous signs besides the ones recorded in this book. But these are written so that you may believe that Jesus is the Messiah, the Son of God, and that by believing in him you will have life.* **John 20:30-31**

## Q: 40. Why is the Bible so big?

A: The Bible is a one-of-a-kind book—and it has a one-of-a-kind message. It tells us the things God wants us to know. It's a story stretching from the creation of the world until eternity, when we will live forever with God in heaven. It's filled with the history of how God and the humans he created have gotten along for thousands of years. It tells us how Jesus came to save us from sin and make us friends with God. And it's a map showing how to follow God's ways. That's a lot to find inside one book! Since the Bible is such a huge book, one of the most important things you can do is to learn your way around. God will be pleased if you learn where some of your favorite Bible stories are written down.

## Learn It
Help your child become familiar with the contents of the Bible. Show how it is split into the Old and New Testaments. Look at the names of the different books and start memorizing the names. You may also want to look up in a concordance or index the names of some favorite Bible characters. Show your child how to find the stories about these people in the Bible.

# Q: 41. How is the Bible different from other books?

A: The Bible is different from most books because it is really many smaller books in one—66, to be exact. More than 40 people helped write the Bible. The Bible was written over a long time— more than 1,500 years. Its writers lived in Asia, Africa, and Europe and wrote in three different languages: Hebrew, Aramaic, and Greek. Yet the Bible is different from all books in an even more important way: It is the totally true Word of God, the Creator of the whole universe. God had the writers put into the Bible exactly what he wanted us to know about himself. He gave us the Bible so we would know how we can trust God's Son, Jesus, and enjoy life that lasts forever with him in heaven. When we want to know how to live close to God, there's no other book like the Bible!

## Share It

Talk with your child about how you have found the Bible to be the most important book you read. How is it different from other books on your shelf? How does it make a difference in your everyday life? Help your child understand that the Bible isn't a book we just listen to or read. It's a book with messages from God, who created us and wants us to learn the very best way to live.

*You have been taught the holy Scriptures from childhood,
and they have given you the wisdom to receive the
salvation that comes by trusting in Christ Jesus.*

**2 Timothy 3:15**

The commandments of the Lord are right, bringing joy to the heart. The commands of the Lord are clear, giving insight to life. **Psalm 19:8**

# Q: 42. Why did God put his words in a book?

A: Suppose you carried a million dollars far into a forest and hid it deep in a mountain cave. If you wanted to be sure that you could find your cash years later, you wouldn't whisper the directions to your dog. You wouldn't trust them to your memory. You would write them down and make a map! God wanted to share with us some very important directions—directions that are even more valuable than a treasure map for digging up a pile of money. God wanted us to be completely clear on how we can be his friend and obey him. So he wrote his instructions in a book to keep them safe. By putting into the Bible everything people need to know, God made sure we couldn't forget or mess up the message.

## Draw It
Find a map (or print one from the Web) that shows clearly how to get to your family's favorite restaurant, park, or vacation destination. Without showing your family members the map, have them draw their own map showing how to get to your special place. Point out—kindly!—that people who tried to follow those maps might get lost. Then show a real map and explain how it is like the Bible. "We can read what other people say about finding God. But God gave us the best directions in the Bible. He wanted us to have clear directions on how to find him and learn about him!"

# Q: 43. How could God write a book?

A: God didn't drop the Bible on us from heaven, wrapped in black leather and decorated with a big bow. Instead, God used people to write his book. But none of the writers just put down their own thoughts. They all wrote God's messages. Sometimes God spoke out loud through prophets and told them to write down what he said. Other times the writers knew in their hearts what they should write. Either way, the message they passed on to us was God's. They spoke—and wrote—so we could know God's words.

## Learn It

Explain that the Bible is different from any other Christian book written now or in the past. Before Jesus came to Earth, God chose people who loved and obeyed him to write down his very own message. After Jesus was born, God chose more people to write about his only Son, and how to believe in him and live for him. This completed what God wanted to tell us.

*Above all, you must understand that no prophecy in Scripture ever came from the prophets themselves or because they wanted to prophesy. It was the Holy Spirit who moved the prophets to speak from God.*

**2 Peter 1:20-21**

*Then the Lord said to Moses, "Write down these words."*
**Exodus 34:27,** NCV

# Q: 44. Who wrote down the words in the Bible?

A: The words of God in the Bible were written down by kings, farmers, fishermen, poets, and even a doctor. The Bible is full of history and poetry and prayers and information. God made the most of each writer's personality and experience. Solomon, for example, shared wisdom God had given him. David sang songs of praise. Prophets like Isaiah and Jeremiah comforted God's people—and warned them against sin. Hosea talked about his broken marriage to teach people about following God. You can think of each writer as an instrument God used to produce a beautiful song. Like the violins and trumpets and flutes and drums in an orchestra, each makes a different sound. Yet each plays a part in God's tune.

## Learn It

Focus on the way in which each Bible writer is special, pointing out that this is one of the Bible's coolest characteristics. To do this, read the different ways God spoke through the following writers about love. Through John: "God is love" (1 John 4:8); Paul: "Let love be your highest goal" (1 Corinthians 14:1); Jeremiah: "I have loved you, my people, with an everlasting love" (Jeremiah 31:3); Hosea: "Plant the good seeds of righteousness, and you will harvest a crop of my love" (Hosea 10:12); and Solomon: "A bowl of soup with someone you love is better than steak with someone you hate" (Proverbs 15:17).

THE BIBLE

# Q: 45. How do we know the Bible is from God?

A: The Bible was written by some of God's best friends—Old Testament heroes like Moses, David, and Solomon, and New Testament followers of Jesus like John and Paul. It's surprising that all these people—who lived in different times and places—could write a book that makes any sense at all. Yet all of the Bible writers agree on hundreds of topics that people argue about. Better yet, the Bible brings us one very special, very clear message about how God wants to save each of us through Jesus. That's a huge way in which we see that the Bible is more than a human book. It's God's Word. He put it together to tell us about himself. The Bible is "inspired by God" or "God-breathed" (NIV). It's packed by God with his powerful message that's worthy of our trust.

**Act It** To make the point that we really need the Bible so that we can know God, hide your Bible behind your back. Then ask, "What would we know about God if he hadn't told us about himself in the Bible?" Some things we wouldn't know: How much God loves us; how God helped people like Noah, Abraham, Moses, Ruth, David, and Esther; how Jesus was born, lived, died, and came back to life; how God wants us to love him and others; and so on. Next, say, "But we can thank God that he did give us a book that tells us what he is like—and how we can be friends with him."

*All Scripture is inspired by God.* **2 Timothy 3:16**

*People are like grass that dies away; their beauty fades
as quickly as the beauty of wildflowers. The grass withers,
and the flowers fall away. But the word of the Lord will
last forever.* **1 Peter 1:24-25**

# Q: 46. The Bible is so old. How could it last so long?

A: When the writers of the Bible wrote down God's words, they didn't have computers or spiral notebooks. They wrote on materials like clay tablets, sheepskin, paper made from tall weeds, and calfskin. The Bible writers handed their writings down to people who copied their work and kept it safe. As handwritten copies wore out, new ones were made and checked letter-by-letter to be sure there were no mistakes. God's people carefully guarded these Bibles in clay pots, caves, and churches so they would last a long time—hundreds and even thousands of years! So many handwritten copies were made that today we have thousands of these copies of different parts of the Bible. Some parts are almost as old as the first writings!

## Compare It

Talk about what might happen if you left a library book out in the rain. Explain that raindrops would ruin the book bit by bit until you owed a chunk of money for a new book. A baseball glove, however, would survive the rain—although it wouldn't be very soft. The people who protected the Bible were smart enough to write on the toughest materials they could find—things like leather and stone. And they didn't leave their Bibles out in the rain!

# Q: 47. Are parts of the Bible make-believe, or is everything true?

A: Even though Jesus lived 2,000 years ago—and many Bible events happened long before he lived—everything in the Bible is real. The Bible writers knew the difference between make-believe and real life, and God gave each of them direction as they wrote carefully about their experiences with him. Luke, for example, was a doctor who used reports from Jesus' closest followers and others who had been with him to write an organized summary of what Jesus said and did (Luke 1:1-4). And John tells us why he wrote carefully about the amazing miracles of Jesus and his awesome rising from the dead: so we could know for sure that when we believe in Jesus, he becomes our Savior (John 20:30-31).

## Learn It

Have your child find in the Bible some of the stories of Jesus' miracles. Like Jesus feeding over 5,000 people from five loaves of bread and two fish (John 6:1-14). Or Jesus walking on water (Matthew 14:25). Or Jesus helping those who were blind to see (Matthew 9:30). Then turn to the book of Acts, in which Luke points out that the events recorded in the Bible "were not done in a corner" (Acts 26:26). Many people saw these events and agreed that they were true.

*The things that happened to those people are examples.*
*They were written down to teach us.*

**1 Corinthians 10:11,** NCV

SLIPPERY SLOPE OF EVIL

*I was jealous of proud people. I saw wicked people doing well. . . . Then I understood what will happen to them. You have put them in danger; you cause them to be destroyed.* **Psalm 73:3, 17-18,** NCV

# Q: 48. What will happen to people who don't obey the Bible?

A: Have you ever seen kids do bad stuff—big and little—and get away with it? Maybe you wish they would stop. Or maybe you wonder if you should join them. Guess what? Anyone who disobeys God's commands in the Bible will come to a sad ending. God won't let people do wrong things forever. In Psalm 73:18 we read, "You put them on a slippery path and send them sliding over the cliff to destruction." We also read, "You are holding my right hand. . . . How good it is to be near God! I have made the Sovereign Lord my shelter" (verses 23, 28). So while you wait for evil to come to an end, keep doing what's right and trusting God to take care of you. It's smart to be on God's side!

## Ask It

Talk over these questions with your child: "When have you been frustrated watching people do bad things—and seem to get away with it?" "What do you think will happen to people who do wrong? Will God stop them right away? Why or why not?" You can dig into the rest of Psalm 73, Lamentations 3:19-33, and the book of Habakkuk for more questions and answers.

# Q: 49. Why is the Bible so hard to understand?

**A:** Suppose you decide to read the Bible from cover to cover. You flip to Genesis 1:1. You read all about Creation. That's not tough. Soon you reach stories you've heard in Sunday school—about Noah and Abraham and Joseph and Moses. They're easy too. Then suddenly you're reading about animal offerings, and directions for making a worship place called a tabernacle, and page after page of strange rules. If you keep going, you stumble over tribes and kings and visions. Yes, the Bible is a big book with lots for us to learn—enough to study for a lifetime, in fact. But the Bible is full of truths you *can* understand. It's packed with commands you can obey today. And it's filled with wisdom you need right now. How do you find the best parts to read? Look up the verses from this book. And ask an adult who knows the Bible well for some other great parts to read!

**Live It** If your child has a tough time grasping the teachings of the Bible, shop for a version that is easier to understand. The Scripture quotations in this book are from the New Living Translation, unless otherwise identified. And for a good family devotional guide, look for the *One Year Book of Josh McDowell's Family Devotions 2*. Like this book, it is a product in the Beyond Belief campaign.

*Your word is a lamp for my feet and a light for my path.*
**Psalm 119:105**

*Jesus replied, " 'You must love the Lord your God with all your heart, all your soul, and all your mind.' This is the first and greatest commandment. A second is equally important: 'Love your neighbor as yourself.' "*

**Matthew 22:37-39**

# Q: 50. Why does the Bible have so many rules?

A: The Bible might seem like it's just full of rules. But the Bible is filled with many other things too. It's packed with words of praise, wise sayings to live by, and loads of history. It tells the story of how God wants to be our friend—and how he sent Jesus to save us. And yes, large sections of the Bible have rules from God, telling us how he wants us to live. But all of the Bible's rules fit under two main rules. Jesus said that the two most important commandments are these: First, "You must love the Lord your God with all your heart, all your soul, and all your mind." And second, "Love your neighbor as yourself." If you remember those two rules and obey them, you'll be obeying all the rules of the Bible!

**Learn It** Put these two important commands of Jesus at the front of your mind. Memorize them together with your family! And for the next several days, encourage one another by pointing out times when you see someone obeying one of these commands. If you see someone being disobedient, encourage that person to think of a way to change—to show love for God or love for a neighbor (which can include parents and siblings).

**Q:**

# 51. Are the Bible's rules old-fashioned?

**A:** Some people think that the Bible's commands must be out-of-date. After all, the Bible was written before cars, computers, and cable TV. Yet reading the Bible is like looking in a mirror. From cover to cover you read stuff that talks about you and your world in its pages. And it's clear that we still need God's rules. Take the Ten Commandments (Exodus 20:1-17). People still have problems with stealing, lying, whining at their parents, and wishing they had their neighbors' toys. Kids on the playground still swear, using God's name disrespectfully. And all of us still forget from time to time to make God more important than anyone or anything else in our lives. God didn't make rules that would only work for a while in the old days—and not be important today. He makes rules that last.

## Share It
Talk with your child about how the "old" rules of the Bible have helped you know how to do the right thing. How have you seen them work for your good?

*Long ago I learned from your rules that you made them to continue forever.* **Psalm 119:152,** NCV

*All he does is just and good, and all his commandments are trustworthy. They are forever true, to be obeyed faithfully.* **Psalm 111:7-8**

# Q: 52. Is the Bible always right?

A: Parents may make mistakes when they help you with your homework. Teachers might have to say, "I don't know" when you ask a question and power up an encyclopedia on the Web to find answers. But there's one source of information that is always available and always has the correct answers: the Bible. In Proverbs 30:5 we read that "every word of God proves true." Second Timothy 3:16 tells us that "all Scripture is inspired by God and is useful to teach us what is true and to make us realize what is wrong in our lives. It straightens us out and teaches us to do what is right." The Bible isn't just a good book full of interesting stories. It's a special book full of God's perfect directions. You can count on the Bible to help you learn how to become friends with God and live the right way!

## Compare It

Explain that the Bible is like a big, sturdy trampoline. You can trust a trampoline to catch you no matter how high you jump. You can trust the Bible to be filled with solid truth from the Lord that will remain standing. It won't change or fall apart, no matter what. It's not like a rickety old chair that will break into pieces if you jump on it. You can always count on the Bible to have correct answers and help you do what's right.

THE BIBLE

121

# Q: 53. Why are there so many different kinds of Bibles?

A: Take a look around your church or a Christian bookstore and you'll see Bibles in all sizes and colors. Flip those Bibles open and you'll find that many have notes to help you study God's Word. Start to read and you'll discover the biggest difference of all: Various Bibles use different words to say the same verse. Even so, the message stays the same. It was written thousands of years ago, mostly in the Hebrew and Greek languages. Today the whole Bible has been written in almost 400 different languages so that people all over the world can understand it. In English there are dozens of versions, but probably just a few are used at your church. Each starts with the original Hebrew and Greek words of the Bible and tries to say them in ways that are clear. That's why different versions of the Bible can sound so different!

## Draw It
Here's an easy way to help your child see why we have so many Bibles. At the top of a sheet of paper, write "God is great!" (Psalm 70:4). Now fill up the paper with all the other ways you can say "great," from "super" and "neato" to "awesome," "funky," "phat," and "cool." As you decorate your sheet, ask, "What does each of these words say about God? Why would we pick one or another to say what he is like?" Explain that Bible translators choose words and phrases that will be easiest for their readers to understand. You can visit Wycliffe Bible Translators at www.wycliffe.org for resources to help your child understand why people of the world need the Bible in their own languages.

GOD IS GREAT!
AWESOME
RADICAL
STUPENDOUS
WOWEE

*Heaven and earth will pass away, but my words will never pass away.* **Matthew 24:35,** NIV

# QUESTIONS ABOUT DIFFERENT RELIGIONS

# 54. Why do people from different religions sometimes fight?

One peek at the TV news tells you that people from different religions don't always get along. Followers of various religions sometimes argue and fight, trying to make others accept their faith. Some even hurt and kill others because they hate people who don't believe the way they do. The Bible shows us a different way of getting people to believe the truth of who Jesus is. We are to tell others about Jesus by explaining how great he is and telling what he has done for us. Here's how Peter explains it: "You were chosen to tell about the wonderful acts of God, who called you out of darkness into his wonderful light" (1 Peter 2:9, NCV). Telling others about Jesus is about giving people reasons to believe—and loving them, not getting angry with them.

## Share It

Talk to your child about opportunities you have had to explain your faith to others—especially people who follow other faiths. How did you give reasons for your faith "in a gentle and respectful way"? How did you show love for the people you talked to?

*Worship Christ as Lord of your life. And if you are asked about your Christian hope, always be ready to explain it. But you must do this in a gentle and respectful way.*

**1 Peter 3:15-16**

*There is one God and one way human beings can reach God. That way is through Christ Jesus. . . . He gave himself as a payment to free all people.*

**1 Timothy 2:5-6,** NCV

# Q: 55. Does my Muslim friend pray to the same God I do?

A: The kids at your school or in your neighborhood probably don't all go to church. At least a few of them might be Muslim, Hindu, Buddhist, or followers of some other religion. Some people say you and your friends all pray to the same God—like you're sending smoke up different chimneys into the same big sky. That sounds cool. But it's not true. Jesus said that his Father is "the only true God" (John 17:3) and that no one gets to God except through him (John 14:6). As a Christian, you know the living, loving God of the Bible. You have an exciting opportunity to share the truth about God with your non-Christian friends!

**Live It** Talk with your child about friends or people you know who haven't trusted Christ because they follow a different faith. Make a plan together to lovingly help them learn about the one true God.

# Q: 56. Do I have to tell people about Jesus?

**A:** Did you know that you have been given the most important job on Earth? Yes, you! If you have trusted in Jesus as your Savior, then God has appointed you to be his messenger. He asks you to spread the Good News that he wants to be friends with everyone in the world—and that he offers forgiveness in Jesus. It's one of the biggest commands Jesus ever gave. He said to "go into all the world and preach the Good News to everyone, everywhere" (Mark 16:15). God doesn't expect you to do the job alone. He has surrounded you with other Christians who have the same job, and Jesus himself promises to always be with you. Telling others about Jesus is a task God commands you to do. But it's also a job you should be glad that God allows you to do for him.

**Act It** Take time to talk and role-play situations likely to come up as your child shares her faith: What should she say? How should she say it? Who should she say it to? The best candidates for one-on-one sharing are people your child sees every day. And the first thing to share is your child's own experience of Christ's love—what Jesus has done for her!

*Go and make disciples of all the nations, baptizing them in the name of the Father and the Son and the Holy Spirit. Teach these new disciples to obey all the commands I have given you. And be sure of this: I am with you always, even to the end of the age.* **Matthew 28:19-20**

*How great you are, O Sovereign Lord! There is no one like you—there is no other God.* **2 Samuel 7:22**

# Q: 57. Does it matter which God people believe in?

**A:** At the time the Bible was written, people worshiped many different gods. Yet those who wrote the Bible said that there is only one God worth believing in. In Exodus 34:14 we read, "You must worship no other gods, but only the Lord, for he is a God who is passionate about his relationship with you." And Acts 4:12 makes it very clear why believing in the God of the Bible matters so much: "Jesus is the only One who can save people. His name is the only power in the world that has been given to save people. We must be saved through him" (NCV). If we really want to know God, we need to know the one real God—and his real plan to make us his friends!

## Ask It

Most children easily accept that God is real, and for most children that means the God of the Bible. But ask your child if she knows anyone who follows a different faith—or who doesn't seem to believe in God at all. Point out that many people say they believe in God but don't follow him, and many others commit their lives to other religions that don't believe Jesus is God's Son. Emphasize that our goal isn't to put down those people— or to stop being friends with them. Our job is to talk to them about Jesus' love for them. We want them to know Jesus can save all of us from sin. He gives joy and peace now. And his death on the cross makes it possible for us to live with God forever someday if we trust in him.

# QUESTIONS ABOUT
## ABOUT
# RIGHT AND WRONG

# Q: 58. Can I decide for myself what's right and wrong?

A: Think about what it would be like to be in the middle of a board game when everyone starts to make up new rules. The game would fall apart. Suddenly the fun would be over. It's exactly like that when people try to decide right and wrong for themselves. Even though it sounds great to make your own rules, people get along far better when we have rules we can count on—rules that don't change, rules made by someone who knows what is best for everyone. Because God is wise and totally unselfish, he makes perfect rules. He makes these rules clear in the Bible. He loves you too much to leave it up to you to pick right and wrong!

## Compare It

Making up our own minds about right and wrong is like being a sailor on the ocean who spins himself in a circle and points anywhere he pleases to decide which way is north. If he doesn't look up into the sky and chart his course by the North Star that God placed there, it won't be long before he's lost. If we ignore the fact that God alone gives us directions for the right way to live, we're going to do a lot of things that are wrong.

*The word of the Lord holds true, and everything he does is worthy of our trust. He loves whatever is just and good, and his unfailing love fills the earth.* **Psalm 33:4-5**

*Your word is a lamp for my feet and a light for my path. I've promised it once, and I'll promise again: I will obey your wonderful laws.* **Psalm 119:105-106**

# Q: 59. Why do we need rules?

A: Roller coaster lovers are smart enough to climb inside coaster cars—not step in front of them. Softball fans know that bats are for pounding balls—not people. Hockey players aim for the other team's goal—not their own. Get it? Even when we do the things we love to do, there are all sorts of rules to help us make the most of our fun. God's commands work the same way. God never makes rules to give us trouble. Jesus, in fact, told us his real goal: "My purpose," he said, "is to give life in all its fullness" (John 10:10). God loves you so much that he gives you his clear commands to show you the very best way to enjoy life.

## Live It
Think together about some rules you have a tough time following. Write down these rules, and for each one, brainstorm three good reasons why that rule exists. How can obeying those rules help you find the "life in all its fullness" that God plans for you?

# Q: 60. Does God punish me when I do wrong?

A: No—and yes. When Jesus died on the cross for you, he canceled forever the punishment you deserve (Isaiah 53:4-9). Because God has forgiven you, there's no longer a need for you to take the blame for your sins. But that doesn't mean you escape the results that come from bad actions. If you don't do your homework, you earn a low grade. If you refuse to wear a bike helmet, sooner or later you bonk your head. If you bug your sister, she's likely to bug you back. So you still get hurt in some ways for doing wrong. And you still need to ask God to forgive you. Yet God's purpose isn't to pound on you. He isn't out to get you for being bad but to teach you that it's always best to choose to do good.

## Share It
Explain that God created families and expects parents to lovingly discipline their children for wrong things they do. Talk about how you feel when your child does wrong. You forgive him for doing wrong—so you get over your anger and ask God to help you not to hold grudges. But you know your child still needs discipline so he or she will want to choose to do what's right the next time. You try to make sure good actions bring good results and bad actions bring bad results.

*My child, don't ignore it when the Lord disciplines you,
and don't be discouraged when he corrects you. For the
Lord disciplines those he loves, and he punishes those he
accepts as his children.* **Hebrews 12:5-6**

*So I advise you to live according to your new life in the Holy Spirit. Then you won't be doing what your sinful nature craves.* **Galatians 5:16**

# Q: 61. Why is it sometimes easier to do things that are wrong than to do what's right?

A: Sit on a chair and try a simple experiment: Slide your bottom off the seat of the chair. What happens? You always fall on the floor. Why? Because you can't undo the power of gravity—the force that pulls you down. It's the same way when it comes to trying in your own strength to overcome the pull of sin. Inside you and every other human being there is a power at work—your sinful nature—that makes it far easier for you to do wrong than right (Galatians 5:17). Yet as a Christian there's an even bigger force at work in you to help you do right: the Holy Spirit. It's the job of the Holy Spirit to help you understand God's commands and obey them. With the Spirit's help, you don't have to do things that are wrong. You can choose to do right!

## Act It

Often we feel like a huge tug-of-war is going on inside of us between the Holy Spirit and our sinful selves. Find a big rope or an old oversize beach towel and go outside for a game of tug-of-war. Then talk about this: "How does it feel when there's a battle between good and evil going on in us? How do we let the Holy Spirit win the tug-of-war?"

## Q: 62. How does God help me choose to do the right thing?

A: God doesn't ask you to do the job of making right choices all alone. He gives you his Word to teach you right from wrong (Psalm 119:105). He shows you how to escape temptation (1 Corinthians 10:13). He also helps in a way you might not have thought of: by promising to meet your every need (Philippians 4:19). That is God's big way of getting rid of your reasons to do wrong. God knows you need friends, for example, and he will show you how to get friends without doing bad stuff to wow them. He knows you need to do well in school, and he will help you study and do your best without cheating. As you live close to God—telling him about your problems and asking him to meet your needs—he will help you. You never have to do bad things to get God's good stuff!

## Share It

How has trusting Jesus to meet your needs helped you make right choices? How has knowing him better changed what you wanted in life and how you went about getting it? Share one or two of these stories with your child. You may also want to discuss the difference between needs and wants. Explain that as we learn to know Jesus better, we start looking at things the way he does. So what we want does change to become what we really need.

*As we know Jesus better, his divine power gives us everything we need for living a godly life.* **2 Peter 1:3**

*If people persecute you because you are a Christian, don't curse them; pray that God will bless them. . . . Never pay back evil for evil to anyone.* **Romans 12:14, 17**

# Q: 63. Why do I sometimes get in trouble for doing the right thing?

A: "No one rules unless God has given him the power to rule," says Paul in Romans 13:1 (NCV). God puts people in charge of you—like parents, teachers, and police—because he plans for them to protect and provide for you. He gives them power to reward good deeds and punish bad ones (Romans 13:3-4). Sometimes, however, people in charge make mistakes and punish good people. Some use their power in wrong ways and hurt people who do right. A few even pick on Christians (Luke 21:17; John 15:20-21). Whether you get in trouble for something you didn't do or just for believing in Jesus, you can obey God by always doing the right thing. You can start by showing respect for the people in charge of you and praying for them!

**Act It** Christian kids can run into trouble not just with adult authorities but with peers. Ask your child if an adult has ever mistakenly accused her of doing wrong— or if another kid has made fun of her for something she said or did because she was trying to follow Jesus. Then role-play how your child can respond to being wrongly accused—or to being picked on for being a believer.

RIGHT AND WRONG

147

## Q: 64. Why do some Christians not act like Christians?

A: There's a big word in the Bible for a person who says he is a Christian but doesn't act like one: *hypocrite* (HIP-uh-krit). It comes from the name for ancient Greek actors famous for the masks they hid behind. It's what Jesus called the religious people who acted good on the outside but were full of sin on the inside (Matthew 23:25-27). He got very angry with them—not for sinning once, twice, or even many times but for pretending to be good when they weren't. Hypocrites act the way they do because they aren't close friends with God. Sometimes hypocrites say they are Christians but do unkind things to other people. When non-Christians see that, they think all Christians are fakes. Being a hypocrite is the exact opposite of what Jesus wants us to be. So don't ever be a pretender. Be a believer who loves Jesus through and through, and show it by the way you act!

**Live It** Help your child name some actions that would be hypocritical for a Christian and wouldn't honor Jesus Christ. Then pray for your family, your church, your pastor, and other Christian leaders—that all believers would stay away from hypocritical actions and "live in a way that brings honor to the Good News of Christ."

*Be sure that you live in a way that brings honor to the Good News of Christ.* **Philippians 1:27,** NCV

# QUESTIONS
## ABOUT
# THE FUTURE

# Q: 65. Does God know what my life will be like when I grow up?

A: David once told God, "You saw me before I was born. Every day of my life was recorded in your book. Every moment was laid out before a single day had passed" (Psalm 139:16). Wow! God knows every deed you will do, every word you will speak, and every breath you will take. God not only knows all about your whole life, but he has an awesome plan for your future. The most important part of his plan is for you to become an excited follower of Jesus, and that's something you can start on right now. Each time you learn about God's clear commands in the Bible— and each time you obey them—you are one step farther along in becoming the person God plans for you to be!

## Learn It
Discuss with your child the fact that God's plan for each of us has two parts. The first is God's clear will for everyone—his "universal will." The second is God's will for each individual—his "specific will." God's universal will is what we learn from God's commands and principles in the Bible. It's where all Christians need to start when we want to do God's will—and it's the most basic place for children to start as they learn to be disciples. Once we begin to obey God's commands for everyone, we're in the right place to find God's will for us as individuals. God reveals this specific part of his plan step-by-step through the Bible, prayer, things that happen, and wise advice from other Christians.

*We can make our plans, but the Lord determines our steps.* **Proverbs 16:9**

*Whatever you do, work at it with all your heart, as working for the Lord.* **Colossians 3:23,** NIV

# Q: 66. Does God care what job I have when I grow up?

A: God cares about everything that's important to you—especially something as huge as the 300 million seconds you will spend working as a grown-up. Perhaps you will get a job in an office or a store, work in a hospital or at a church, or start your own business. You may become a farmer or carpenter, travel as a salesperson, work at home caring for a family, or become a missionary. Whatever work you choose to do as an adult, this is one of the biggest decisions you will ever make. And God has a plan for you. In Ephesians 2:10 we read, "We are God's masterpiece. He has created us anew in Christ Jesus, so that we can do the good things he planned for us long ago." God made you his special work of art—a one-of-a-kind bundle of gifts—and he decided long ago what good work you would do!

## Share It
Share with your child how you see God's plan for you at work in how you spend your adult life. Talk about the gifts and abilities God has given you to help you do your job. Help your child identify some gifts and abilities that may help her know what work God wants her to do someday.

# Q: 67. Will God tell me what will happen in my future?

A: There's no doubt that God knows about your future. He has an awesome plan for your life. The big question is how much he plans to tell you—and when. Actually, God wants to tell you a whole lot about your future, but he is too wise to tell you all of it at once. He will tell you only what you need to know exactly when you can handle it! For example, you don't need to know in third grade—or even in sixth grade—where you'll go to college, what you'll do for a job, if you'll get married, or when and where you'll retire! God lovingly chooses to keep your future a secret. But as you ask him to help you make right choices—starting now—he will show you his plan for your life one step at a time!

## Draw It
Have your child draw a picture entitled "My Future Is in God's Hands." Give him free rein to draw whatever he thinks his future might look like. Ask your child to tell you about each part of the picture. Then pray for God's wisdom as you and your child trust God to direct every path.

*Trust in the Lord with all your heart; do not depend on your own understanding. Seek his will in all you do, and he will direct your paths.* **Proverbs 3:5-6**

There is wonderful joy ahead, even though it is necessary for you to endure many trials for a while. These trials are only to test your faith, to show that it is strong and pure.

**1 Peter 1:6-7**

# Q: 68. Why does God let bad things happen to me sometimes?

**A:** Sometimes bad things happen to you because of your own poor choices—like gulping pool water because you jumped in over your head without knowing how to swim. Some hurtful things come because of other people's bad choices—like getting hit by a driver talking on a cell phone. And other bad stuff—like sickness, storms, and earthquakes—just happens because we live in a world that's not perfect. When you're hurt or sad, remember this: Jesus made a wonderful promise to be with you through anything and everything (Matthew 28:20). And he will use the bad things that happen to help you trust him more. He wants you to know that you can count on him no matter what you go through!

## Live It

Explain that the bad things, big or small, that happen to us daily cause feelings of sadness. Read Romans 12:15 together: "When others are happy, be happy with them. If they are sad, share their sorrow." Then pray for someone who is feeling sad—pray that God would show you how to comfort that person. Remind your child that bad things will happen on this Earth, but in heaven there will be no more sadness.

THE FUTURE

## 69. Can God make bad things turn out okay?

A: When bad things happen to you, God promises to do a surprising thing: make good come out of bad! When you love God, he makes everything in your life happen the way he plans it (Romans 8:28). That doesn't mean that God will always help you get right out of bed when you're sick. And he won't help you remember math facts you didn't take the time to learn. Sometimes God does quickly save you from your troubles, but not always. But there is one good thing God plans to bring out of every bad thing you face: He wants to help you learn to think and act like his Son, Jesus (Romans 8:29). God always helps you and holds you in his arms when you hurt. And the very best thing he is doing for you is making sure that everything that happens in your life helps you become more like Jesus!

**Live It** Do you know anyone who is facing a difficult time right now? Make a plan as a family to show that person God's wonderful love and care.

*We know that God causes everything to work together for the good of those who love God and are called according to his purpose for them. For God knew his people in advance, and he chose them to become like his Son.*

**Romans 8:28-29**

# QUESTIONS
# ABOUT
# CHURCH

# Q: 70. Why do we go to church?

A: When you trusted Jesus to be your Savior, God made you part of the church. No, he didn't turn you into a brick. He made you a member of what the Bible calls the "body of Christ" (1 Corinthians 12:12-13, 26-27). He joined you to a huge group—all of Jesus' followers from around the world. You probably get together often with part of that group—the church family that attends worship services in your local church building. We need each other! The Holy Spirit gives each of us a job to do to help each other grow closer to Jesus. He gives us jobs like serving, encouraging, giving, teaching, and leading (Romans 12:6-8; 1 Corinthians 12:4-11). And just like your body doesn't work well without all its parts, the body of Christ (the church) doesn't work well unless each of us joins in!

## Compare It
God put us together in the church to keep our friendship with him warm and bright. Explain to your child that the church is like a roaring campfire. A coal kept in the center of the flame will glow all night. But a coal pushed off to the side goes out and its warmth quickly fades. The people in a church family need to stay together just like those coals need to stick close together.

*We are all parts of his one body, and each of us has different work to do. And since we are all one body in Christ, we belong to each other, and each of us needs all the others.* **Romans 12:5**

*We should not stop gathering together with other believers, as some of you are doing. Instead, we must continue to encourage each other even more.*

**Hebrews 10:25,** GW

# Q: 71. Why does church last so long?

A: That's a funny question. Have you ever heard anyone wonder why parties last so long? Probably not. God didn't plan for us to be miserable at church. He wants every get-together among Christians to be a time to celebrate! Church is a total bore only when leaders up front or people in the pews forget why they're there. A worship service at church is a special time to enjoy our friendship with each other and, most of all, with God. If you ever start to snooze at church, wake yourself up with this fact: The Bible commands you to hang out with God's people so you can keep encouraging each other to become better and better friends with him!

## Learn It

Talk with your child about what's exciting at church. How do the songs, the Bible lessons, the prayers, the service projects, and so on, help each of you love Jesus more? Every activity your family participates in at church should take you and your children beyond belief. It should take you from a mere familiarity with the truths of the Christian faith into a life-changing love relationship with God and your fellow believers. If you aren't confident that you or your children are being led step-by-step into a real, lifelong friendship with Jesus, you can be part of a revolution in your church. Visit www.beyondbelief.com to learn how.

# Q: 72. My friend doesn't go to church. What should I do?

A: A friend who doesn't go to church could be a Christian who is missing out on the awesome, growing friendship she could have with Jesus—and some of his followers. Or maybe a friend who picks soccer or sleeping in over Sunday school has never trusted Jesus. Either way, church might not sound like much fun to your friend. But as this kid watches you live your life close to Jesus, sooner or later she will wonder how you got so tight with God. And that's your chance to invite your friend to come along to worship, Sunday school, or another activity—not just to meet your great friends or be part of a group, but to get to really know and believe in Jesus!

## Live It

Who in your child's world needs to meet Jesus—maybe in a deep way, maybe for the first time? What can you do as a family to help that friend connect with Jesus? You might want to plan some activities at your house in which your child invites both Christian and non-Christian friends. Perhaps you can offer to pick up a neighboring child for Sunday school. Or your child could invite a friend to an after-school Bible club.

*You were chosen to tell about the wonderful acts of God, who called you out of darkness into his wonderful light. At one time you were not a people, but now you are God's people.* **1 Peter 2:9-10,** NCV

# QUESTIONS ABOUT
# DEATH AND HEAVEN

# Q:

## 73. Why did my grandma die when the Bible says that Christians will live forever?

# A:

No one escapes death, not even Christians. Younger people sometimes die because of accidents or sickness. Older people can die from accidents or disease too, but many die simply because their bodies wear out. We feel sad when people die, because we miss them. But here's the important fact: Death isn't the end for us. Even when we die, the most important part of us keeps living. It's the part we can't see—our "spirit" or "soul." That part of Christians will live forever. Jesus said, "I am the resurrection and the life. Those who believe in me, even though they die like everyone else, will live again" (John 11:25). What a promise! Everyone who trusts in Jesus will live forever!

## Share It
Explain to your child how the death of a Christian close to you brought you a mixture of sadness and joy—sadness that your loved one was physically gone, but joy that he or she will live forever with Jesus. Let your child express her own feelings related to the loss of a life. It could be a church friend, a neighbor, or a relative.

*I [Jesus] tell you the truth, whoever hears what I say and believes in the One who sent me has eternal life. That person will not be judged guilty but has already left death and entered life.* **John 5:24, NCV**

THE NEW ETERNAL ME!

*Our earthly bodies, which die and decay, will be different when they are resurrected, for they will never die. . . . They are natural human bodies now, but when they are raised, they will be spiritual bodies. For just as there are natural bodies, so also there are spiritual bodies.*

**1 Corinthians 15:42, 44**

# Q: 74. What will I look like in heaven?

A: Guess what? You'll still be you—only better! The Bible says your spirit will live forever. But it also promises you'll get a new body to live in. Right now we all have "earthly bodies" that die (1 Corinthians 15:42). But in heaven we will get "spiritual bodies" that last forever (1 Corinthians 15:42, 44). God will take the bodies we have now and "change them into glorious bodies like his own, using the same mighty power that he will use to conquer everything, everywhere" (Philippians 3:21). Your new body will be filled with the same power that raised Jesus from the dead. It will be like the body Jesus got after he came back to life—not because it comes with a beard and long hair but because it won't ever break or wear out—or die!

## Compare It

Find something around your home that needs fixing and set it in front of your child. Getting a new body in heaven, you can explain, is like completely remaking that broken object. If you could make all new parts—and fashion them so they would last forever—then you would have something like our new heavenly bodies. The broken object would be the same—but better than ever!

DEATH AND HEAVEN

# Q: 75. Will everybody go to heaven?

**A:** There's only one way people can go to heaven when they die. It's by trusting Jesus while they are alive. Everyone who trusts Jesus will live forever in heaven with God. People who say no to God's gift of forgiveness will live away from God and his people forever (John 5:24-29; Matthew 25:31-46). God's biggest desire is for people to turn away from their sins—the bad things they do—and come back to him. They can do this by trusting Jesus as their Savior, admitting he is the only one who can forgive them and help them become friends with God. We should be eager to tell others about Jesus, so we can bring as many people with us to heaven as we can!

**Act It** The people in the verse above thought that Jesus was slow about coming back to Earth (Matthew 24:30-31). But any delay in his return is time for more people to repent. God wants all people to turn away from their sins and follow him. Act out the word *repent* by having your child walk away from you, then turn around and walk back to you. Explain, "That's what it means to repent. When you sin, it's like walking away from God. Then God commands you to turn around—to leave your sinful beliefs and actions and come back to him, believing and acting the way he wants you to. That's what God wants all of us to do!" A moving end to this exercise would be to exchange places and act out your own repentance by coming back to your child.

*The Lord isn't really being slow about his promise to return, as some people think. No, he is being patient for your sake. He does not want anyone to perish, so he is giving more time for everyone to repent.* **2 Peter 3:9**

*And so we will be with the Lord forever.*

**1 Thessalonians 4:17**, NIV

# Q: 76. How long will we be in heaven?

**A:** That's an easy one. Forever! One of the most famous verses in the Bible says this: "For God so loved the world that he gave his only Son, so that everyone who believes in him will not perish but have eternal life" (John 3:16). The word *eternal* means something that will never end. Jesus promised that he was going to prepare a place for us. He said, "I will come and get you, so that you will always be with me where I am" (John 14:3). Here's the hard part. We can't begin to get our brains to understand the fact that we will live in heaven always and forever. But we can get this much: Eternal life isn't just about having lungs that work for a really long time. It's about having a heart that will love forever the Lord of the universe—your best-ever friend, Jesus!

## Compare It

Think together of the best moments you have had as a family. Explain, "That's just a little taste of what heaven might be like. What makes heaven even better is that God himself will be there, and he will make it a place we will enjoy being forever and ever." Then read Revelation 21:3-4: "I heard a loud shout from the throne, saying, 'Look, the home of God is now among his people! He will live with them, and they will be his people. God himself will be with them. He will remove all of their sorrows, and there will be no more death or sorrow or crying or pain. For the old world and its evils are gone forever.'" Heaven isn't just about eternal life. It's about eternal love and happiness!

# Q: 77. How do I know I'm going to heaven?

**A:** Good question! In fact, Jesus' best friends asked him the same thing. Jesus said there is just one way to get to his Father's home in heaven—and he is it! Jesus declared that *he* is the way. It may seem strange to think of a person as a path, but Jesus is saying, "If you want to get to heaven, the only way to get there is by believing in me." Jesus made a very special promise to his followers. He said, "I assure you, those who listen to my message and believe in God who sent me have eternal life" (John 5:24). He was saying that if we believe in God and follow Jesus, we'll live forever! Those are directions you can count on to get you to God's home!

## Draw It

Explain that Jesus has sent each of us an invitation to heaven. Say, "We are invited to believe in Jesus and trust him to give us eternal life. Going to live with Jesus in heaven forever will be like going to a party that never ends!" Have your child choose some words from John 14:6 or John 5:24 to design and decorate an invitation to God's eternal home.

*Jesus told him, "I am the way, the truth, and the life. No one can come to the Father except through me."*

**John 14:6**

# Index of Bible Verses

Genesis 1:31          QUESTION 1

Exodus 34:27          QUESTION 44

2 Samuel 7:22         QUESTION 57

Psalm 19:7, 11        QUESTION 4
Psalm 19:8            QUESTION 42
Psalm 32:2-3          QUESTION 3
Psalm 33:4-5          QUESTION 58
Psalm 62:8            QUESTION 23
Psalm 73:3, 17-18     QUESTION 48
Psalm 86:5, 10        QUESTION 15
Psalm 100:3           QUESTION 14
Psalm 103:12          QUESTION 13
Psalm 111:7-8         QUESTION 52
Psalm 119:105         QUESTION 49
Psalm 119:105-106     QUESTION 59
Psalm 119:152         QUESTION 51
Psalm 139:1           QUESTION 19

Proverbs 3:5-6        QUESTION 67
Proverbs 4:18-19      QUESTION 9
Proverbs 16:9         QUESTION 65

Isaiah 53:5           QUESTION 10

Habakkuk 1:13         QUESTION 5

Matthew 22:37-39      QUESTION 50
Matthew 24:35         QUESTION 53
Matthew 26:59-60      QUESTION 25

Matthew 28:5-6      QUESTION 35
Matthew 28:19-20    QUESTION 56

Mark 1:35           QUESTION 17

Luke 2:52           QUESTION 28

John 1:11-12        QUESTION 30
John 1:18           QUESTION 2
John 5:24           QUESTION 73
John 10:32-33       QUESTION 29
John 14:6           QUESTION 77
John 14:13-14       QUESTION 24
John 14:16-17       QUESTION 36
John 15:15          QUESTION 39
John 20:30-31       QUESTION 40
John 21:24          QUESTION 33

Romans 1:4          QUESTION 34
Romans 3:22         QUESTION 12
Romans 3:25         QUESTION 7
Romans 5:8          QUESTION 16
Romans 6:23         QUESTION 6
Romans 8:11         QUESTION 31
Romans 8:28-29      QUESTION 69
Romans 8:38         QUESTION 20
Romans 12:5         QUESTION 70
Romans 12:14, 17    QUESTION 63

1 Corinthians 10:11     QUESTION 47
1 Corinthians 15:3-4    QUESTION 32
1 Corinthians 15:42, 44 QUESTION 74

Galatians 4:7       QUESTION 8
Galatians 5:16      QUESTION 61
Galatians 5:22-23   QUESTION 37

Ephesians 3:17          **QUESTION 27**

Philippians 1:27        **QUESTION 64**

Colossians 3:23         **QUESTION 66**

1 Thessalonians 4:17    **QUESTION 76**

1 Timothy 2:5-6         **QUESTION 55**

2 Timothy 3:15          **QUESTION 41**
2 Timothy 3:16          **QUESTION 45**

Hebrews 4:15-16         **QUESTION 26**
Hebrews 10:25           **QUESTION 71**
Hebrews 12:5-6          **QUESTION 60**

James 4:7-8             **QUESTION 38**

1 Peter 1:6-7           **QUESTION 68**
1 Peter 1:17            **QUESTION 21**
1 Peter 1:18-19         **QUESTION 18**
1 Peter 1:24-25         **QUESTION 46**
1 Peter 2:9-10          **QUESTION 72**
1 Peter 3:15-16         **QUESTION 54**
1 Peter 5:7             **QUESTION 22**

2 Peter 1:3             **QUESTION 62**
2 Peter 3:9             **QUESTION 75**
2 Peter 1:20-21         **QUESTION 43**

1 John 1:8-9            **QUESTION 11**

# Index of Topics by Question Number

Bible 39–53
Church 70–72
Death and heaven 73–77
Devil 38
Forgiveness 10–13
Future 65–69
God 1–2
God's love 14–21
Holy Spirit 36–37
Jesus 25–35
Prayer 22–24
Religions 54–57
Right and wrong 58–64
Sin 3–9

BELIEF.

# Incite A CROSSCULTURE™ Revolution

Here is a foundational family of products to transform a generation into passionate followers of Christ who know why they believe what they believe.

**Josh McDowell**
& Bob Hostetler

## BE CONVINCED OF WHY YOU BELIEVE

### *Beyond Belief to Convictions* Book to Adults

Having Christian convictions means being so thoroughly convinced that Christ and his Word are both objectively true and relationally meaningful that you act on your beliefs regardless of the consequences. *Beyond Belief* contains the blueprint for a revolution in the lives of young people. It will help you lead them to a real encounter with God and transform them into passionate followers of Christ.
***Beyond Belief to Convictions*** SC: 0-8423-7409-4

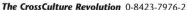

### *The CrossCulture Revolution* Book to Adults

Why call for a revolution? Josh and Ron cite at least three compelling reasons: (1) Despite the efforts of the church, Christian schools, and Christian families, the vast majority of our kids lead lives virtually no different from non-Christians; (2) our kids consistently make wrong moral choices; and (3) upon leaving home, our young people do not remain in the church. The authors offer a spiritual revolution manifesto for the church and family to raise up a "cross culture"—a transformed generation of passionate followers of Christ.
***The CrossCulture Revolution*** 0-8423-7976-2

### *In Search of Certainty* Book to Adults

Statistics are alarming. Eighty-eight percent of the U.S. population does not believe in a moral absolute. Postmodernism has undermined the concept of absolute truth in the past generation, leaving even Christians groping for meaning and certainty in their lives. This book exposes the irrationalities of atheistic positions, showing that God is real and truth is absolute, and only trust in him can provide certainty that life has meaning and fulfillment. An excellent book to give to a seeker friend. ***In Search of Certainty*** 0-8423-7972-X

# BE CONVINCED OF WHY YOU BELIEVE

## *Josh McDowell's Youth Devotions 2*
## *Josh McDowell's Family Devotions 2*
### to Youth/Families

"We are not fighting against people made of flesh and blood, but against the evil rulers and authorities of the unseen world . . ." (Ephesians 6:12, NLT). More than ever our young people need a spiritual defense. This second installment of Josh's best-selling youth and family devotions offer 365 daily devotional encounters with the true Power Source to strengthen your family spiritually and provide your young people with a resource that will help them combat today's culture. *Josh McDowell's Youth Devotions 2*  0-8423-4096-3
*Josh McDowell's Family Devotions 2*  0-8423-5625-8

## *The Deceivers* Book to Youth

Written in the popular NovelPlus format, this book combines the adventures of Sarah Milford and Ryan Ortiz and their search for meaning, along with Josh's insights found in sections called "The Inside Story."

In dramatic fashion *The Deceivers* explains that unless Christ is who he claims to be—the true Son of God—then his offer to redeem us and provide meaning to life can't be real. This book presents not only the compelling evidence for the deity of Christ but also how God's plan is to transform us into a new creature with an intimate relationship with him.  *The Deceivers* 0-8423-7969-X

## *Children Demand a Verdict* Book to Children

Children need clear and direct answers to their questions about God, the Bible, sin, death, etc. Directed to children ages 7–11, this question-and-answer book tackles 77 tough issues with clarity and relevance, questions such as: Why did God make people? How do we know Jesus was God? How could God write a book? Is the Bible always right? Are parts of the Bible make-believe? Why did Jesus die? Did Jesus really come back to life? Does God always forgive me? Why do people die? Will I come back to life like Jesus?
*Children Demand a Verdict*  0-8423-7971-1

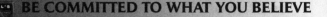

## BE CHANGED BY WHO YOU BELIEVE

### Workbook for Adult Groups

Combining interactive group discussion with daily activities, this workbook helps you overcome the distorted views of Christ and biblical truth held by most children and youth today. It will help you lead them to a fresh encounter with the "God who is passionate about his relationship with you" (Exodus 34:14, NLT). The daily activities reveal a credible, real, and relevant Christ you can share with each family member.

The workbook study provides 8 solid group teaching sessions for the weekly at-home assignments to model the message before others. *Belief Matters Workbook* Wkbk: 0-8423-8010-8  Ld. Gd: 0-8423-8011-6

### Workbook for Youth Groups

When your students reject the world's counterfeit way of life, what will life in Christ really be like for them? This 8-session course helps each of your students realize that new life in Christ is about transformation, about belonging to Christ and one another in his Body, about knowing who they really are, and about living out their mission in life.

*The Revolt Workbook* is an 8-session youth group interactive course followed up with students engaging in two daily exercises per week. This study is the perfect follow-up to the companion *Revolt Video Series*. *The Revolt Workbook*  Wkbk: 0-8423-7978-9  Ld. Gd: 0-8423-7979-7

### Workbook for Children's Groups

To raise up the next generation of committed followers of Christ, we must start when they are young. These workbooks for children grades 1–3 and grades 4–6 present the foundational truth of why Christ came to earth. Written in simple terms, they lead your children to realize why doing wrong has separated them from God and why only Christ can bring them into a close family relationship with God.

In 8 fun-filled sessions, your children will learn why Christ is the true way and all other ways are false. These sessions lead children to a loving encounter with the "God who is passionate about his relationship with [them]" (Exodus 34:14, NLT).

*True or False Workbook* Younger Wkbk: 0-8423-8012-4  Older Wkbk: 0-8423-8013-2  Ld. Gd: 0-8423-8014-0

**Contact your Christian Supplier to obtain these resources
and begin the revolution in your home, church, and community.**